I0411104

114TH CONGRESS
1ST SESSION

S. _____

To amend the FAA Modernization and Reform Act of 2012 to provide guidance and limitations regarding the integration of unmanned aircraft systems into United States airspace, and for other purposes.

IN THE SENATE OF THE UNITED STATES

Mr. MARKEY introduced the following bill; which was read twice and referred to the Committee on _____

A BILL

To amend the FAA Modernization and Reform Act of 2012 to provide guidance and limitations regarding the integration of unmanned aircraft systems into United States airspace, and for other purposes.

1   *Be it enacted by the Senate and House of Representa-*

2 *tives of the United States of America in Congress assembled,*

3 **SECTION 1. SHORT TITLE.**

4   This Act may be cited as the "Drone Aircraft Privacy

5 and Transparency Act of 2015".

6 **SEC. 2. FINDINGS.**

7   Congress finds the following:

1   (1) On February 14, 2012, President Obama

2   signed the FAA Modernization and Reform Act of

3   2012 (Public Law 112–95; 49 U.S.C. 40101 note)

4   into law, and sections 331 through 336 of such Act

5   require the Federal Aviation Administration to fully

6   integrate government, commercial, and recreational

7   unmanned aircraft systems, commonly known as

8   "drones", into United States airspace by October

9   2015.

10   (2) Unmanned aircraft systems have tradition-

11   ally been used almost exclusively overseas by mili-

12   tary and security organizations; however, State and

13   local governments, businesses, and private individ-

14   uals are increasingly using unmanned aircraft sys-

15   tems in the United States, including deployments for

16   law enforcement operations.

17   (3) As the technology advances and the cost de-

18   creases—unmanned aircraft systems are already or-

19   ders of magnitude less expensive to purchase and op-

20   erate than piloted aircraft—the market for Federal,

21   State, and local government and commercial un-

22   manned aircraft systems is rapidly growing.

23   (4) It has been estimated there could be as

24   many as 30,000 unmanned aircraft systems in the

25   sky in the United States by 2020.

1   (5) There will no doubt be many beneficial ap-
2 plications of this technology, for as Secretary of
3 Transportation Ray LaHood said in a statement on
4 March 7, 2012, "Unmanned aircraft can help us
5 meet a number of challenges, from spotting wildfires
6 to assessing natural disasters.".

7   (6) However, there also is the potential for un-
8 manned aircraft system technology to enable
9 invasive and pervasive surveillance without adequate
10 privacy protections, and currently, no explicit pri-
11 vacy protections or public transparency measures
12 with respect to such system technology are built into
13 the law.

14   (7) Federal standards for informing the public
15 and protecting individual privacy with respect to un-
16 manned aircraft systems are needed.

17 **SEC. 3. GUIDANCE AND LIMITATIONS REGARDING UN-**
18   **MANNED AIRCRAFT SYSTEMS.**

19   (a) IN GENERAL.—Subtitle B of title III of the FAA
20 Modernization and Reform Act of 2012 (Public Law 112–
21 95; 49 U.S.C. 40101 note) is amended by adding at the
22 end the following new sections:

23 **"SEC. 337. PRIVACY STUDY AND REPORT.**

24   "(a) STUDY.—The Secretary of Transportation, in
25 consultation with the Secretary of Commerce, the Chair-

1 man of the Federal Trade Commission, and the Chief Pri-
2 vacy Officer of the Department of Homeland Security,
3 shall carry out a study that identifies any potential threats
4 to privacy protections posed by the integration of un-
5 manned aircraft systems into the national airspace sys-
6 tem, including any potential violations of the privacy prin-
7 ciples.

8   "(b) REPORT.—Not later than 180 days after the
9 date of the enactment of this section, the Secretary of
10 Transportation shall submit a report on the study con-
11 ducted under subsection (a) to—

12   "(1) the Committee on Transportation and In-
13   frastructure, the Committee on Energy and Com-
14   merce, and the Committee on Homeland Security of
15   the House of Representatives; and

16   "(2) the Committee on Commerce, Science, and
17   Transportation, the Committee on Environment and
18   Public Works, and the Committee on Homeland Se-
19   curity and Governmental Affairs of the Senate.

20 **"SEC. 338. RULEMAKING.**

21   "As part of the rulemaking process required under
22 section 332(b)(1) and the final rule adopted under such
23 section, the Secretary of Transportation shall establish
24 procedures to ensure that the integration of unmanned

1 aircraft systems into the national airspace system is done

2 in compliance with the privacy principles.

3 **"SEC. 339. DATA COLLECTION STATEMENTS AND DATA**

4 **MINIMIZATION STATEMENTS.**

5   "(a) IN GENERAL.—Beginning on the date of the en-

6 actment of this section, the Secretary of Transportation

7 may not approve, issue, or award any certificate, license,

8 or other grant of authority to operate an unmanned air-

9 craft system in the national airspace system unless the

10 application for such certificate, license, or other grant of

11 authority includes—

12   "(1) a data collection statement in accordance

13   with the requirements of subsection (b) that provides

14   reasonable assurance that the applicant will operate

15   the unmanned aircraft system in accordance with

16   the privacy principles; and

17   "(2) in the case of such an unmanned aircraft

18   system that is to be operated by a law enforcement

19   agency or a law enforcement agency contractor or

20   subcontractor, a data minimization statement in ac-

21   cordance with the requirements of subsection (c)

22   that provides reasonable assurance that the appli-

23   cant will operate the unmanned aircraft system in

24   accordance with the privacy principles.

1   "(b) DATA COLLECTION STATEMENT.—A data col-
2 lection statement under subsection (a), with respect to an
3 unmanned aircraft system, shall include information iden-
4 tifying—

5   "(1) the individuals or entities that will have
6   the power to use the unmanned aircraft system;

7   "(2) the specific locations in which the un-
8   manned aircraft system will operate;

9   "(3) the maximum period for which the un-
10   manned aircraft system will operate in each flight;

11   "(4) whether the unmanned aircraft system will
12   collect information or data about individuals or
13   groups of individuals, and if so—

14   "(A) the circumstances under which the
15   system will be used; and

16   "(B) the specific kinds of information or
17   data the system will collect about individuals or
18   groups of individuals and how such information
19   or data, as well as conclusions drawn from such
20   information or data, will be used, disclosed, and
21   otherwise handled, including—

22   "(i) how the collection or retention of
23   such information or data that is unrelated
24   to the specified use will be minimized;

1   "(ii) whether such information or data

2   might be sold, leased, or otherwise pro-

3   vided to third parties, and if so, under

4   what circumstances it might be so sold or

5   leased;

6   "(iii) the period for which such infor-

7   mation or data will be retained; and

8   "(iv) when and how such information

9   or data, including information or data no

10   longer relevant to the specified use, will be

11   destroyed;

12   "(5) the possible impact the operation of the

13 unmanned aircraft system may have upon the pri-

14 vacy of individuals;

15   "(6) the specific steps that will be taken to

16 mitigate any possible impact identified under para-

17 graph (5), including steps to protect against unau-

18 thorized disclosure of any information or data de-

19 scribed in paragraph (4), such as the use of

20 encryption methods and other security features that

21 will be used;

22   "(7) a telephone number or electronic mail ad-

23 dress that an individual with complaints about the

24 operation of the unmanned aircraft system may use

25 to report such complaints and to request confirma-

1   tion that personally identifiable data relating to such

2   individual has been collected;

3   "(8) in a case in which personally identifiable

4   data relating to an individual has been collected, a

5   reasonable process for the individual to request to

6   obtain such data in a timely and an intelligible man-

7   ner;

8   "(9) in a case in which a request described in

9   paragraph (8) is denied, a process by which the indi-

10   vidual may obtain the reasons for the denial and

11   challenge the denial; and

12   "(10) in a case in which personally identifiable

13   data relating to an individual has been collected, a

14   process by which the individual may challenge the

15   accuracy of such data and, if the challenge is suc-

16   cessful, have such data erased or amended.

17   "(c) DATA MINIMIZATION STATEMENT.—A data

18 minimization statement described in this subsection, with

19 respect to an unmanned aircraft system operated by a law

20 enforcement agency, contractor, or subcontractor de-

21 scribed in subsection (a)(2), shall detail the applicable—

22   "(1) policies adopted by the agency, contractor,

23   or subcontractor, as the case may be, that—

24   "(A) minimize the collection by the un-

25   manned aircraft system of information and data

1   unrelated to the investigation of a crime under

2   a warrant;

3   "(B) require the destruction of such infor-

4   mation and data, as well as of information and

5   data collected by the unmanned aircraft system

6   that is no longer relevant to the investigation of

7   a crime under a warrant or to an ongoing

8   criminal proceeding; and

9   "(C) establish procedures for the method

10   of such destruction; and

11   "(2) audit and oversight procedures adopted by

12   the agency, contractor, or subcontractor, as the case

13   may be, that will ensure that the agency, contractor,

14   or subcontractor, as the case may be, uses the un-

15   manned aircraft system in accordance with the pa-

16   rameters outlined in the data collection statement

17   and the statement required by this subsection.

18 **"SEC. 340. DISCLOSURE OF APPROVED CERTIFICATES, LI-**

19   **CENSES, AND OTHER GRANTS OF AUTHORITY.**

20   "(a) IN GENERAL.—The Administrator of the Fed-

21 eral Aviation Administration shall make available on the

22 public Internet website of the Federal Aviation Adminis-

23 tration in a searchable format—

24   "(1) the approved certificate, license, or other

25   grant of authority for each unmanned aircraft sys-

1   tem awarded a certificate, license, or other grant of

2   authority to operate in the national airspace system,

3   including any such certificate, license, or other grant

4   of authority awarded prior to the date of the enact-

5   ment of this section;

6   "(2) information detailing where, when, and for

7   what period each unmanned aircraft system will be

8   operated;

9   "(3) information detailing any data security

10   breach that occurs with regard to information col-

11   lected by an unmanned aircraft system; and

12   "(4) in the case of a certificate, license, or

13   other grant of authority awarded on or after the

14   date of the enactment of this section to operate an

15   unmanned aircraft system in the national airspace

16   system, the data collection statement described in

17   section 339(b) and, if applicable, the data minimiza-

18   tion statement described in section 339(c) required

19   with respect to such unmanned aircraft system.

20   "(b) DEADLINE.—The Administrator shall complete

21   the requirements under subsection (a) with regard to each

22   unmanned aircraft system—

23   "(1) in the case of a certificate, license, or

24   other grant of authority awarded before the date of

1   the enactment of this section, not later than 90 days

2   after such date of enactment; and

3   "(2) in the case of a certificate, license, or

4   other grant of authority awarded on or after the

5   date of the enactment of this section, as soon as is

6   practicable after the date of approval of such certifi-

7   cate, license, or other grant of authority.

8 **"SEC. 341. WARRANTS REQUIRED FOR GENERALIZED SUR-**

9   **VEILLANCE.**

10   "(a) IN GENERAL.—A governmental entity (as de-

11 fined in section 2711 of title 18, United States Code) may

12 not use an unmanned aircraft system or request informa-

13 tion or data collected by another person using an un-

14 manned aircraft system for protective activities, or for law

15 enforcement or intelligence purposes, except pursuant to

16 a warrant issued using the procedures described in the

17 Federal Rules of Criminal Procedure (or, in the case of

18 a State court, issued using State warrant procedures) by

19 a court of competent jurisdiction, or as permitted under

20 the Foreign Intelligence Surveillance Act of 1978 (50

21 U.S.C. 1801 et seq.).

22   "(b) EXCEPTION.—

23   "(1) IN GENERAL.—Subsection (a) shall not

24   apply in exigent circumstances (as defined in para-

25   graph (2)).

1   "(2) EXIGENT CIRCUMSTANCES DEFINED.—Ex-

2   igent circumstances exist when—

3   "(A) a law enforcement entity reasonably

4   believes there is an imminent danger of death

5   or serious physical injury; or

6   "(B) a law enforcement entity reasonably

7   believes there is a high risk of an imminent ter-

8   rorist attack by a specific individual or organi-

9   zation and the Secretary of Homeland Security

10   has determined that credible intelligence indi-

11   cates there is such a risk.

12   "(3) REQUIRED DOCUMENTATION.—In the case

13   of a person operating an unmanned aircraft system

14   under the exception for exigent circumstances under

15   paragraph (1), documentation justifying the excep-

16   tion shall be submitted to the Secretary of Transpor-

17   tation not later than 7 days after the date of the rel-

18   evant unmanned aircraft system flight.

19   "(4) INFORMATION OR DATA UNRELATED TO

20   EXIGENT CIRCUMSTANCES.—A person operating an

21   unmanned aircraft system under the exception for

22   exigent circumstances under paragraph (1) shall

23   minimize the collection by the unmanned aircraft

24   system of information and data unrelated to the exi-

25   gent circumstances. If the unmanned aircraft system

1   incidentally collects any such information or data
2   while being operated under that exception, the per-
3   son operating the unmanned aircraft system shall
4   destroy the information and data.

5   "(5) PROHIBITION ON INFORMATION SHAR-
6   ING.—A person may not intentionally divulge infor-
7   mation collected in accordance with this section with
8   any other person, except as authorized by law.

9   "(6) PROHIBITION ON USE AS EVIDENCE.—If
10   information has been collected by means of use of an
11   unmanned aircraft system, no part of the contents
12   of that information and no evidence derived from
13   that information may be received in evidence in any
14   trial, hearing, or other proceeding in or before any
15   court, grand jury, department, officer, agency, regu-
16   latory body, legislative committee, or other authority
17   of the United States, a State, or a political subdivi-
18   sion thereof unless that information is collected in
19   accordance with this section.".

20   (b) DEFINITIONS.—Section 331 of the FAA Mod-
21   ernization and Reform Act of 2012 (Public Law 112–95;
22   49 U.S.C. 40101 note) is amended—

23   (1) by redesignating paragraphs (4) through
24   (9) as paragraphs (7) through (13);

14

1   (2) by redesignating paragraph (3) as para-

2   graph (4);

3   (3) by inserting after paragraph (2) the fol-

4   lowing:

5   "(3) LAW ENFORCEMENT.—The term 'law en-

6   forcement' means—

7   "(A) any entity of the United States or of

8   a State, or political subdivision thereof, that is

9   empowered by law to conduct investigations of

10   or to make arrests for offenses; and

11   "(B) any entity or individual authorized by

12   law to prosecute or participate in the prosecu-

13   tion of such offenses."; and

14   (4) by inserting after paragraph (4), as redesig-

15   nated by paragraph (2), the following:

16   "(5) PRIVACY PRINCIPLES.—The term 'privacy

17   principles' means the principles described in Part

18   Two of the Organization for Economic Co-operation

19   and Development guidelines titled 'Annex to the

20   Recommendation of the Council of 23rd September

21   1980: Guidelines Governing The Protection Of Pri-

22   vacy And Transborder Flows Of Personal Data',

23   adopted by the Organization for Economic Co-oper-

24   ation and Development on September 23, 1980.

1   "(6) PRIVACY PROTECTIONS.—The term 'pri-

2   vacy protections' means protections that relate to

3   the use, collection, and disclosure of information and

4   data about individuals and groups of individuals.".

5 **SEC. 4. ENFORCEMENT.**

6   (a) PROHIBITED CONDUCT.—

7   (1) IN GENERAL.—It shall be unlawful for a

8   person to operate an unmanned aircraft system in a

9   manner that is not in accordance with the terms of

10   a data collection statement submitted under section

11   339(a)(1) of the FAA Modernization and Reform

12   Act of 2012, as added by section 3, or in a manner

13   that violates any portion of the final rule required

14   under section 332(b)(1) of such Act insofar as such

15   portion relates to the procedures described in section

16   338 of such Act.

17   (2) REGULATIONS.—The Commission may pro-

18   mulgate regulations in accordance with section 553

19   of title 5, United States Code, to carry out para-

20   graph (1) with respect to persons, partnerships, and

21   corporations described in subsection (b)(3).

22   (b) ENFORCEMENT BY FEDERAL TRADE COMMIS-

23 SION.—

24   (1) UNFAIR OR DECEPTIVE ACTS OR PRAC-

25   TICES.—A violation of subsection (a) or the regula-

1 tions promulgated under such subsection shall be

2 treated as a violation of a regulation under section

3 18(a)(1)(B) of the Federal Trade Commission Act

4 (15 U.S.C. 57a(a)(1)(B)) regarding unfair or decep-

5 tive acts or practices.

6   (2) POWERS OF COMMISSION.—The Commis-

7 sion shall enforce subsection (a) and the regulations

8 promulgated under such subsection in the same

9 manner, by the same means, and with the same

10 powers and duties as though all applicable terms

11 and provisions of the Federal Trade Commission Act

12 (15 U.S.C. 41 et seq.) were incorporated into and

13 made a part of this Act, and any violator shall be

14 subject to the penalties and entitled to the privileges

15 and immunities provided in the Federal Trade Com-

16 mission Act.

17   (3) APPLICABILITY.—Paragraphs (1) and (2)

18 shall apply—

19   (A) with respect to persons, partnerships,

20   and corporations over which the Commission

21   has jurisdiction under section 5(a)(2) of the

22   Federal Trade Commission Act (15 U.S.C.

23   45(a)(2)) (except to the extent such person,

24   partnership, or corporation is a law enforce-

25   ment contractor or subcontractor); and

(B) notwithstanding such section, with respect to air carriers and foreign air carriers.

(c) ACTIONS BY STATES.—

(1) CIVIL ACTIONS.—In any case in which the attorney general of a State, or an official or agency of a State, has reason to believe that an interest of the residents of that State has been or is threatened or adversely affected by an act or practice in violation of subsection (a) or a regulation promulgated under such subsection, or by the operation of an unmanned aircraft system in violation of the terms of a data minimization statement submitted under section 339(a)(2) of the FAA Modernization and Reform Act of 2012, as added by section 3, the State may bring a civil action on behalf of the residents of the State in an appropriate State court or an appropriate district court of the United States to—

(A) enjoin the violation;

(B) enforce compliance with such subsection, regulation, or statement;

(C) obtain damages, restitution, or other compensation on behalf of residents of the State; or

1   (D) obtain such other legal and equitable

2   relief as the court may consider to be appro-

3   priate.

4   (2) NOTICE.—Before filing an action under this

5   subsection against a person, partnership, or corpora-

6   tion over which the Commission has jurisdiction

7   under section 5(a)(2) of the Federal Trade Commis-

8   sion Act (15 U.S.C. 45(a)(2)) (except to the extent

9   such person, partnership, or corporation is a law en-

10   forcement contractor or subcontractor) or an air car-

11   rier or foreign air carrier, the attorney general, offi-

12   cial, or agency of the State involved shall provide to

13   the Commission a written notice of that action and

14   a copy of the complaint for that action. If the attor-

15   ney general, official, or agency determines that it is

16   not feasible to provide the notice described in this

17   paragraph before the filing of the action, the attor-

18   ney general, official, or agency shall provide written

19   notice of the action and a copy of the complaint to

20   the Commission immediately upon the filing of the

21   action.

22   (3) AUTHORITY OF THE COMMISSION.—

23   (A) IN GENERAL.—On receiving notice

24   under paragraph (2) of an action under this

1   subsection, the Commission shall have the
2   right—

3   (i) to intervene in the action;
4   (ii) upon so intervening, to be heard
5   on all matters arising therein; and
6   (iii) to file petitions for appeal.

7   (B) LIMITATION ON STATE ACTION WHILE
8   FEDERAL ACTION IS PENDING.—If the Commis-
9   sion or the Attorney General of the United
10   States has instituted a civil action for violation
11   of subsection (a) or a regulation promulgated
12   under such subsection (referred to in this sub-
13   paragraph as the "Federal action"), no State
14   attorney general, official, or agency may bring
15   an action under this subsection during the
16   pendency of the Federal action against any de-
17   fendant named in the complaint in the Federal
18   action for any violation as alleged in that com-
19   plaint.

20   (4) RULE OF CONSTRUCTION.—For purposes of
21   bringing a civil action under this subsection, nothing
22   in this Act or any amendment made by this Act
23   shall be construed to prevent an attorney general,
24   official, or agency of a State from exercising the
25   powers conferred on the attorney general, official, or

1   agency by the laws of that State to conduct inves-

2   tigations, administer oaths and affirmations, or com-

3   pel the attendance of witnesses or the production of

4   documentary and other evidence.

5   (d) PRIVATE RIGHT OF ACTION.—

6   (1) IN GENERAL.—A person injured by an act

7   in violation of subsection (a) or the regulations pro-

8   mulgated under such subsection, or by the operation

9   of an unmanned aircraft system in violation of the

10   terms of a data minimization statement submitted

11   under section 339(a)(2) of the FAA Modernization

12   and Reform Act of 2012, as added by section 3, may

13   bring in an appropriate State court or an appro-

14   priate district court of the United States—

15   (A) an action to enjoin such violation;

16   (B) an action to recover damages for ac-

17   tual monetary loss from such violation, or to re-

18   ceive up to $1,000 in damages for each such

19   violation, whichever is greater; or

20   (C) both such actions.

21   (2) INTENTIONAL VIOLATIONS.—If the defend-

22   ant committed a violation described in paragraph

23   (1), and intended to do so, the court may increase

24   the amount of the award to an amount equal to not

1 more than 3 times the amount available under para-

2 graph (1)(B).

3   (3) COSTS.—The court shall award to a pre-

4 vailing plaintiff in an action under this subsection

5 the costs of such action and reasonable attorney's

6 fees, as determined by the court.

7   (4) LIMITATION.—An action may be com-

8 menced under this subsection not later than 2 years

9 after the date on which the person first discovered

10 or had a reasonable opportunity to discover the vio-

11 lation.

12   (5) NONEXCLUSIVE REMEDY.—The remedy pro-

13 vided by this subsection shall be in addition to any

14 other remedies available to the person.

15   (e) SUITS AGAINST GOVERNMENTAL ENTITIES.—

16 Notwithstanding the Federal Trade Commission Act (15

17 U.S.C. 41 et seq.), a suit under subsection (c) or (d) may

18 be maintained against a governmental entity.

19   (f) LICENSE REVOCATION.—The Federal Aviation

20 Administration shall revoke the certificate, license, or

21 other grant of authority to operate an unmanned aircraft

22 system if such system is operated in a manner that—

23   (1) is not in accordance with the terms of—

24   (A) a data collection statement submitted

25   under subsection (a)(1) of section 339 of the

1   FAA Modernization and Reform Act of 2012,

2   as added by section 3; or

3   (B) a data minimization statement sub-

4   mitted under subsection (a)(2) of such section;

5   or

6   (2) violates any portion of the final rule re-

7   quired under section 332(b)(1) of such Act insofar

8   as such portion relates to the procedures described

9   in section 338 of such Act, as added by section 3.

10   (g) VIOLATIONS.—Each day on which each un-

11 manned aircraft system is operated in violation of sub-

12 section (a), or the regulations promulgated under such

13 subsection, or the terms of a data minimization statement

14 submitted under section 339(a)(2) of the FAA Moderniza-

15 tion and Reform Act of 2012, as added by section 3, shall

16 be treated as a separate violation.

17   (h) DEFINITIONS.—In this section:

18   (1) AIR CARRIER; FOREIGN AIR CARRIER.—The

19   terms "air carrier" and "foreign air carrier" have

20   the meanings given those terms in section 40102 of

21   title 49, United States Code.

22   (2) COMMISSION.—The term "Commission"

23   means the Federal Trade Commission.

24   (3) LAW ENFORCEMENT.—The term "law en-

25   forcement" has the meaning given such term in sec-

1   tion 331 of the FAA Modernization and Reform Act

2   of 2012, as amended by section 3.

3   (4) STATE.—The term "State" means each of

4   the several States, the District of Columbia, each

5   commonwealth, territory, or possession of the United

6   States, and each federally recognized Indian tribe.

7   (5) UNMANNED AIRCRAFT SYSTEM.—The term

8   "unmanned aircraft system" has the meaning given

9   such term in section 331 of the FAA Modernization

10   and Reform Act of 2012 (49 U.S.C. 40101 note).

11   **SEC. 5. MODEL AIRCRAFT PROVISION.**

12   Nothing in this Act may be construed to apply to

13   model aircraft (as defined in section 336(c) of the FAA

14   Modernization and Reform Act of 2012 (Public Law 112–

15   95; 49 U.S.C. 40101 note)).